145271

Does a Mouse Have a House?

by Anne Miranda

Bradbury Press   New York

Maxwell Macmillan Canada   Toronto
Maxwell Macmillan International
New York   Oxford   Singapore   Sydney

Bradbury Press
Macmillan Publishing Company
866 Third Avenue
New York, NY 10022

Maxwell Macmillan Canada, Inc.
1200 Eglinton Avenue East
Suite 200
Don Mills, Ontario M3C 3N1

Macmillan Publishing Company is part of the Maxwell
Communication Group of Companies.

Printed and bound in Hong Kong by South China Printing Company (1988) Ltd.
First edition
10 9 8 7 6 5 4 3 2 1

The text of this book is set in Galliard.
Book design by Julie Quan

ABOUT THE ART: The illustrations are cut-paper collages. First the artist textured
the paper with ink. Then she cut shapes and glued them to create the images.

LIBRARY OF CONGRESS CATALOGING-IN-PUBLICATION DATA
Miranda, Anne.
Does a mouse have a house? / by Anne Martin Miranda.—1st ed.
p.   cm.
ISBN 0-02-767251-4
1. Animals—Habitations—Juvenile literature. [1. Animals—
Habitations.] I. Title.
QL756.M57   1994
591.56'4—dc20   93-20587

To Mary Jane Martin

Home sweet home to a bee
is a hive in a tree.

A spider's place
is a web like lace.

The desert owl makes a practice of nesting in a prickly cactus.

The giant panda, black and white,
sleeps among bamboo at night.

Pink flamingos flock together
at shallow lakes in sunny weather.

Penguins must make
ice suffice.

Many a toothy crocodile
swims the ancient River Nile.

The hippopotamus can float
along the river like a boat.

Camels dwell in desert places;
they stop to drink at lush oases.

A mallard is fond
of a lily-pad pond.

The turtle lives well
in its hard, painted shell.

Elephant and zebra roam
across the plain that is their home.

Around a coral reef, the fishes
swim wherever each fish wishes.

The snaky, fangy moray eel
hides in places that conceal.

A beaver's home
is a mud-and-stick dome.

Does a mouse
have a house?

I think mice
have homes that are nice!